Last Summer with Maizon

Last Summer with Maizon

JACQUELINE WOODSON

HARCOURT BRACE & COMPANY

Orlando Atlanta Austin Boston San Francisco Chicago Dallas New York

Toronto London

This edition is published by special
arrangement with Dell, a division of Bantam
Doubleday Dell Publishing Group, Inc.

Grateful acknowledgment is made to Dell,
a division of Bantam Doubleday Dell
Publishing Group, Inc. for permission to
reprint *Last Summer with Maizon* by
Jacqueline Woodson, cover illustration by
Leo and Diane Dillon. Text copyright
© 1990 by Jacqueline Woodson; cover
illustration copyright © 1990 by Leo and
Diane Dillon.

Printed in the United States of America

ISBN 0-15-302251-5

3 4 5 6 7 8 9 10   071   97 96 95 94

For Linda, Teresa, and Michelle

C H A P T E R 1

MARGARET dangled her legs over the edge of the fire escape and flipped to a clean page in her diary.

"I haven't written in a long time," she began, "but now with this Blue Hill thing and all, I feel like I should. Maizon took a test in May. If she passes, she's going to go to this big private school in Connecticut.

"Every night I pray she doesn't get accepted."

She heard a rumble and looked out toward the bridge. The train was a long shadow in the twilight, creeping slowly across water she couldn't see. She watched it for a moment, then stood up and searched the block for Maizon. Lights flickered on and off in the brownstones across from her. A hot summer breeze blew out of the darkness.

Margaret sat down again and continued writing.

"I don't know why Maizon has to go to some dumb boarding school anyway. The schools in Brooklyn are fine. And when I say Blue Hill out loud, it makes me think of someplace sad and cold all the time. Maizon said it probably isn't so cold in Connecticut. She doesn't know about the sad part though. She said without a best friend, it'll probably get a little lonely. Ms. Dell said we shouldn't go counting our chickens because we're not even sure if Maizon's going to get accepted or not. Every day, we wait for a letter. I feel like I'm on one of those balance beams we have in gym class—balancing between today and tomorrow."

Margaret closed the book and climbed back inside just as her father came into the living room. She looked at the small blue suitcase he was carrying and frowned.

"Just some tests," he said softly, sitting down beside her on the window ledge. Another train rumbled and somewhere in the distance a baby was crying.

"How long will the hospital keep you this time?" Margaret asked. She remembered her last visit and started to tremble.

Her father rested his chin on the top of her head. "Until they find out what's making this old ticker act the way it's acting. Could be a week. Could be a day." His voice trailed off. Margaret put her arms around him.

"Don't let them take the life out of you, Daddy," she whispered. She remembered her father's dark, handsome face looking shriveled and old beneath the hospital covers.

"What makes you think your daddy's gonna let some-

2

thing like that happen?" He sat up straight and Margaret felt a cold spot where his chin had been.

"Listen here, Margaret . . ." he began, taking her chin in his hands and gently pulling her face toward him.

Behind the slow smile he gave her he looked tired and worried. The wrinkles between his thick eyebrows cut deeply into his forehead.

"You gonna have to hold this family together while I'm gone, take care of your mama and Li'l Jay."

Margaret nodded.

A shadow crossed her father's face. "It might take a little while for me to get back on my feet after all these silly tests they gonna run. But don't worry your pretty little head about that. It would take a lot for one of them skinny plastic tubes to bring this six-footer down."

Her father brushed a stray hair out of her eyes. "Why does your mama think she needs to hide all of this pretty hair?"

Margaret smiled and shrugged, then turned a little so her father could undo her braid. His hands felt strong and sure.

"There now. Pretty head of hair like that needs to hang free." He kissed her on the forehead.

Margaret ran her fingers through her hair. It hung to her shoulders in thick waves.

"Where's that crazy Maizon?" he asked, leaning back out of the window and taking a quick look down the block.

"She's coming."

"Maybe she'll even get here before tomorrow," her father laughed.

Her mother came out of the bedroom, with Li'l Jay following behind her. At fourteen months, walking was still new to him and he was constantly following whoever let him.

"Margaret, what'd I tell you about messing with your hair?"

Margaret started to speak but her father caught her eye and winked.

"I was just telling her to look after you two while I'm gone," he said.

"And who's going to look after Margaret?" her mother teased.

"Jay!" Li'l Jay shouted, throwing his bottle across the floor.

They laughed.

"Daddy, will you be home for the block party?"

Her father scooped her up the way he had done when she was young and swung her toward the ceiling.

Margaret laughed and punched his shoulders.

"Block party! Hah!" He sat her down gently and hugged her. "We're going to have a Tory family reunion!"

"Yay!" Li'l Jay said, spinning in a circle and hurling himself onto the floor. He giggled and sat up.

She watched from the window as her mother helped her father into a cab, then climbed in beside him. The car crawled slowly down the empty street, signaled once, then turned the corner.

"Daddy . . ." she said, realizing he hadn't answered

4

her question. "Good-bye, Daddy." Margaret hated the way the words sounded in the now quiet apartment.

"Li'l Jay!" she yelled.

"Jay," he repeated, toddling into the living room with a pan in his hand. The feet of his baggy pajamas dragged behind him.

"When Maizon gets here, you're going to bed," Margaret warned. "No crying, either."

"Maizon!" Jay repeated, banging the pot against the hardwood floor.

"Bed," Margaret said, turning back to the window and pressing her hands to her ears. A hot breeze blew in over his noise.

"Man, it's hot tonight!" She pulled her shirt away from her chest and blew down onto her skin. Where was Maizon, anyway? "Li'l Jay, stop that noise!"

The room fell silent. Margaret turned to Li'l Jay. His bottom lip quivered.

"Oh, Jay," she said, lifting him into her arms. "I'm sorry." She carried him over to the window. The pot clattered to the floor.

They sat on the radiator and stared out past the brownstones at the bridge. Past the lights, Manhattan loomed up dark and shadowy in the distance. The train rumbled by slowly and Li'l Jay began to whine.

"Sounds like it's in pain, doesn't it?" Li'l Jay pressed his head against her shoulder. "Probably creeping across that bridge for the millionth time."

"Twain," he said, drifting off to sleep.

5

Margaret stared out into the growing night for a long time.

"You look like Mary and Baby Jesus," Maizon yelled up. Li'l Jay woke with a start.

"It's about time!" Margaret yelled back. In the near-darkness she could only make out Maizon's Afro and dark dress. She carried Li'l Jay to his crib, then ran to hide her diary.

"What'd you do to your hair? It's scary," Maizon said when Margaret opened the door.

"Me?! Your grandmother's going to skin you alive when she finds out you left the house looking like that," Margaret said. "And with her make-up and earrings too? Maizon, I know you've lost your mind!"

Maizon smiled and sauntered past her. She wore a red and black dress with a black and a red pocket on either side and a red tie at the collar. Her small Afro looked strange against the two red circles she had blushed onto her cheeks. Huge gold-hoop earrings dragged down her earlobes and her black eye-liner was crooked.

She turned to give Margaret a better look and smiled, showing off.

"Margaret . . . Margaret . . . Margaret . . ." Maizon said, dragging out the name in a phony, grown-up tone. "Are you so corny that you don't know this is what everybody's wearing in the city? Everybody!" She twirled again and pulled out a magazine she had tucked underneath her dress.

"Look!" She said, opening to a page and pointing to a picture of a black woman modeling an outfit identical to her own. "This is where I saw the dress first. My grand-mother made this one exactly like it, and now I'm the first girl in Brooklyn to have it! You want me to ask her to make you one?"

"Nah, I don't really like it." Margaret stared longingly at the black sleeves gathered around Maizon's wrists.

"You just don't like it 'cause I got it first!" Maizon declared. She went over to the refrigerator and looked into the fruit bin. "I hate pears," she said, sucking her teeth and reaching for one.

"I don't like red and black together—especially in the summer when it's so hot outside," Margaret said.

Maizon looked the pear over carefully. "This pear is all bruised up," she said, taking a bite. "You should tell your mother to buy her pears at Ocasio's. They have the fresh-est ones. Jefferson Avenue Market has good apples, but their pears aren't so great."

"My mother doesn't have time to shop, between work-ing and worrying about my father and everything. Not everyone can sit around like your grandma and make dresses!"

Maizon took another bite and frowned. Margaret turned away from her and flipped angrily through the magazine.

"Well then, ask your mother to give us money and we'll do the shopping," Maizon suggested.

"I don't like to ask her a lot of things because it seems like she's always crying. That makes me cry. And Li'l Jay's always crying!" Margaret yelled.

Maizon sucked her teeth again. "God, sorry I asked!"

She stared at her pear. "Isn't your daddy getting any better?"

"They've gone to the hospital for tests. He's going to have to stay there. He looks skinnier too." Margaret put her elbows on the table. Didn't Maizon understand anything?

"You gonna go visit him?"

"They said maybe I shouldn't go anymore because I get too upset. I always start crying. I hate the way those white sheets swallow him up. It scares me."

"You want me to go to the hospital with you?"

Margaret nodded. "I do, but only family can visit him. If you could go, maybe I wouldn't start crying."

"I wish the stupid hospital people didn't know your family. Then I could make believe I was your sister or something."

Margaret took a pear from the refrigerator and began cutting away the peel.

"Hey! That's the best part!" Maizon said, grabbing the peel. She tossed her core into the garbage can.

"I hate that part." Margaret pushed the small green pile across the counter to her, glad Maizon wasn't mad at her for yelling.

"Where's Junior?" Maizon asked with her mouth full.

"One of these days my mother's gonna hear you call him that and kick you out of the house."

"I know, but Li'l Jay sounds dumb. No one calls your dad 'Big Jay.'"

"Yeah, I know." She handed the rest of her peel to Maizon. "*Li'l Jay's* asleep."

8

"Can you go outside?"

"Only if Ms. Dell and Hattie are there. Did you see them when you were coming upstairs?"

"No, but they're probably just waiting until it gets a little cooler out. Anyway, it's only eight-thirty."

"Maizon . . . you think you can show me how to do the Snake?"

"The Snake," she screeched. "Where have you been, Margaret? Under a rock? That dance has been dead for ages!"

"Oh, you ain't so smart, Maizon Singh!" she shouted. "You think you know everything, but you don't! You don't know anything!" Margaret screamed, running into the living room. She buried her face in one of the couch pillows and cried. After a moment, Maizon tiptoed in and sat beside her.

CHAPTER 2

"I'M SORRY, MARGARET," she whispered. "Sometimes I act like I know so much."

Margaret sniffed, angry at herself for being ready to forgive her so quickly.

"I gotta stay in this dumb old house all the time and take care of Li'l Jay while you get to go all around Brooklyn. I just sit in the window and watch everything go by. I wish my daddy wasn't so sick, so it could be like it was before. I don't know anything anymore!" She buried her head in the pillow again.

"The Bismarck is the latest dance, Margaret," Maizon said. "I just learned it last week. I was going to show it to you. Honest!"

"For real, Maizon?" Margaret sat up.

"Yeah. It's not so hard, either."

"How does it go?"

"I need the right music," Maizon said, getting up from the couch.

Margaret went over to the stereo and flipped through the stack of records on the stand beside it.

"I have 'Do That Dance Again' in a giant forty-five," she said. "Is that a good record for it?"

"Yeah! That's the rap I learned it to."

A long time ago, Margaret realized Maizon knew a lot more about things than she did. Now she wanted to ask her who had taught her how to do the Bismarck, where she had learned. But the answers Maizon gave always made her jealous, so she didn't ask. Instead, she put the record on the turntable and turned the volume down so Li'l Jay wouldn't wake up.

"First you move your feet like this," Maizon said, clicking her heels together.

Margaret followed halfheartedly.

"Now put your arms out and move your shoulders. Like this."

Maizon moved so easily, she didn't even have to listen to the rhythm. "Try it," she said.

Margaret stood across from Maizon and tried to move like she did, but her feet got in the way of the rest of her and she stumbled. Maizon giggled and Margaret glared at her. Sometimes it didn't seem fair. Maizon had everything.

"Do it slowly at first."

She slowed down a little and Margaret followed her.

"Look!" Maizon said. "You can do it almost as good as me!"

They played the record a few more times and practiced.

"I'm tired," Maizon said when Margaret started to begin the record for the fifth time.

"Me too." She turned off the stereo and followed Maizon over to the couch.

"I'm sorry I made you cry before, Margaret."

"You didn't make me cry," Margaret said, leaning back against a blue corduroy pillow. "I did it to myself. I thought about sad things and just started crying." That was almost true, she thought. And even if it wasn't, it sounded good.

"Sad things like what?" Maizon asked, curling up at the other end.

"Like not knowing things."

"Yeah, that is pretty sad. Sometimes I wish we could be like Ms. Dell. People say she can see into the future because her eyes are such a strange shade of blue."

"Her eyes *are* strange. I wonder why Hattie didn't get eyes like her mother."

"Hattie can't 'see' things the way Ms. Dell can," Maizon said. "I heard she used to be able to. But after her baby died, she lost a little bit of her mind. That's why only Ms. Dell knows the future now. People say it's a special gift, direct from God to her."

"Where do you think that little bit of Hattie's mind went?"

Maizon thought for a moment. "Maybe to heaven with

her baby. Grandma says when you lose a baby, it's like losing a piece of yourself."

"Ms. Dell takes good care of her."

"Ms. Dell takes good care of everyone. That's why she's here. Once I heard Grandma asking her what brought her to Madison Street, and you know what Ms. Dell said?"

Margaret moved a little closer because Maizon's voice had dropped to a whisper. "What?"

"She said that space in her mind that tells her when things are going to happen said, 'Ms. Dell, you better get yourself out of the South and come to Madison Street quick, 'cause that block is going to be needing you!' "

"For real, Maizon?"

Maizon nodded. "Yup. And when you got a gift like Ms. Dell's, you pass it on. Since Hattie doesn't have it anymore, Ms. Dell is going to pass it on to someone else. Sure hope it's me!"

"I don't know if I'd want to know the future. Sounds like it could get scary sometimes."

"Yeah," Maizon said. "But there are some things I wouldn't mind knowing."

"Like what?"

"Like if I'm going to get into Blue Hill or not. I mean, how long ago did I take that test?"

"Three months and four days," Margaret said.

Maizon glanced at her, surprised. "How can you remember that?"

" 'Cause it was the same day Daddy had the first heart attack, remember? I came home from school and you and

Ms. Dell and Hattie were all sitting on the steps. That's when I knew something was wrong, because Hattie and Ms. Dell were baby-sitting Li'l Jay even though it wasn't Mama's work day. And then you were telling me how hard the test was but Ms. Dell told you to be quiet and let me go on upstairs."

Maizon cut her off. "And then you went upstairs and your mama was there and she was crying, right?"

"Uh huh," Margaret said softly, remembering seeing tears in her mother's eyes for the first time in her life.

"That's what I'm talking about, Margaret. See, like what if we knew things the way Ms. Dell does? We could change things. Make them not happen or happen."

"I guess so," Margaret said.

Maizon was thinking hard now. She furrowed her brow and pressed her palm against her mouth.

"Margaret!" she said all of a sudden. "Let's find out!"

"How?"

"Let's sneak the information out of Ms. Dell!"

Margaret rolled her eyes. "Ms. Dell is too smart for that, Maizon."

"We're smart."

"Not smarter than Ms. Dell."

"Come on, Margaret. Ms. Dell's been living downstairs for ten years. She sees and knows everything. Your mother tells her things she doesn't tell you. I bet my grandmother does too. Everybody trusts her."

Margaret shook her head. "That's because she doesn't blab."

Maizon folded her arms. "Forget it, then. We'll never

know. When September comes and I go away, we won't be prepared for it. We won't be prepared for anything that ever happens 'cause we won't know.''

"So?"

"So you want to never know anything?"

Margaret thought about the Bismarck. "I want to know *some* things."

"Then let's go," Maizon said, pulling Margaret's arm. "Let's milk them out of Ms. Dell."

"I don't know, Maizon . . .''

"Why not?"

"Maybe we're not supposed to know the future."

Maizon got up quickly.

"Don't you want to know how your daddy is? How your daddy *really* is?"

"I don't know, Maizon."

"I know how you feel, Margaret," Maizon said softly. Margaret knew she was telling the truth. "It's like when you see a car accident and you really want to see who's inside and how bad they're hurting, but you don't want to look because you know looking might make you feel worse, right?"

Margaret nodded. That was exactly how she felt.

"But then you go away without looking, Margaret," Maizon said in the same low voice, "and you spend the rest of your life wondering."

"I guess," Margaret said.

"Then come on." Maizon ran to the window and leaned out. "They're out there now. Let's just sit on the stoop with them and try to get a little info."

"What about Li'l Jay?" Margaret asked. She had to get out of this.

"What about him? He needs some air. He sleeps too much. And you know how crazy Ms. Dell is over him. We can plant him on her lap and"—she snapped her finger—"we're there!"

"I have to comb my hair." In a second Maizon was behind her, wrapping it into a French braid.

"This hair sure is wild," she said longingly. By the time she was done, Margaret had run out of excuses.

Maizon changed Li'l Jay's diaper while Margaret searched for her ribbon. Then they descended the six flights down to Ms. Dell and Hattie.

↘C H A P T E R   3↙

"**I** was wondering when you two were going to bring your tails down here. Always up in that apartment messing around with I don't know what," Ms. Dell said, putting her glass of iced tea down beside her before taking Li'l Jay from Maizon and sitting him on her lap.

Maizon caught Margaret's eye and winked.

Ms. Dell was a big woman, and her flowered cotton housedress stretched tightly across her fleshy thighs.

"We just sit and wonder about things," Maizon said.

"What do two eleven-year-olds have to wonder about?" Hattie asked incredulously.

"Same thing as a nineteen-year-old," Maizon said.

Hattie smirked and her high cheekbones jutted up toward her eyes. Her skin was dark brown like her mother's and looked smooth under the yellow streetlights.

19

"I know you two got something up those sleeves, 'cause there ain't no time Frick and Frack get together— winter, spring, summer or fall—that they don't have something planned. Always something up those sleeves." Hattie leaned back and winked at her mother. Her brown eyes were always sad, which made her look like she was about to cry even when she laughed.

"Hattie," Ms. Dell said, bouncing Li'l Jay on her knee. He squealed and drooled onto his pajama top. "You remember when Margaret first moved around here and Maizon come around in her Indian outfit talking 'bout she heard there was some new girl on the block with a 'forked tongue'?"

"Yeah, I remember. And Margaret peeping out her window scared as I don't know what." Hattie laughed.

"I wasn't scared," Margaret said. "I just couldn't come outside."

"You girls gonna miss each other when you're no longer together," Ms. Dell warned.

Margaret felt Maizon's elbow in her side.

"No longer together?" Maizon said too innocently. "Where are we going?"

"Wherever," Ms. Dell said. "Everybody's got to go somewhere."

"Margaret's not going anywhere!" Maizon stood up, threw her head back and shouted, "Margaret and Maizon! Friends forever!"

"Girl, stop all that shoutin' and set yourself down. It's not Margaret going anywhere. She's gonna take care of her mother—" Ms. Dell stopped abruptly and stared down at the pavement.

"How do you know, Ms. Dell?" Maizon asked quickly. "What do you mean Margaret has to take care of her mother?"

"I don't know anything, child," Ms. Dell said, rubbing Li'l Jay's head. "Don't listen to me talking outta my hat."

"You do know," Maizon accused. "You have those eyes. People say, Ms. Dell . . . they say you know."

"You heard her, Maizon," Hattie said. "She said she doesn't know. Let it be already."

Maizon turned to Hattie. "But we need to know. We have to know what's going to happen."

"Why?" Hattie asked. "Why do you need to know *everything,* Maizon?"

Maizon glared at her. Margaret knew she only tolerated Hattie because she was Ms. Dell's daughter and Hattie only tolerated Maizon because she was Margaret's friend. "So we can plan for it. For whatever."

"When it happens, you'll know," Hattie said, and they both knew that meant the subject was closed. Margaret sighed, relieved. She had always liked Hattie.

The stoop grew quiet. The smell of rain was in the air and Margaret listened as a low roll of thunder rumbled above them.

"We blew it," Maizon whispered. Margaret nodded. "We could have milked her if Hattie wasn't around."

Ms. Dell shifted Li'l Jay and took a long sip from her frosted glass. Her blue eyes wandered slowly from Maizon to Margaret.

"I know what they have up those sleeves, Hattie. They're on an information hunt."

"Not gonna find any 'cyclopedias over here," Hattie said, tight-lipped.

Maizon yawned and turned to Margaret.

"We gonna go shopping for school clothes tomorrow?"

Margaret nodded.

"School clothes? In July?"

Margaret leaned against Hattie's shoulder. "We want to get the same outfits, and if we wait too long, we won't be able to find two of everything."

"Yeah," Maizon said, "we're going to tell people we're cousins." She turned to Ms. Dell. "If I don't get into Blue Hill, we're going to be in the same class!"

"Oh, you will?"

"Yeah, Ms. Peazle's," Maizon said, wrinkling her nose. "I hear she's a biddy!" Maizon raced down the block before Ms. Dell could scold her. She stopped a few houses down.

"Call me tomorrow!" she yelled, then waved and continued down the block. Margaret watched her turn into her brownstone.

Ms. Dell looked up at the sky and whistled. "Gonna come a hard rain. Gonna last a while too. Better get those rubbers out if you planning on doing some walking tomorrow."

A yellow cab pulled up to the curb and Ms. Tory leaned forward to pay the driver. From what Margaret could see, her mother looked worn and tired. Margaret's heart leapt.

"Gonna learn about strength this summer, Margaret," Ms. Dell said softly. But Margaret was off the stoop and halfway to the cab by the time Ms. Dell got the words out.

⚞ C H A P T E R   4 ⚟

I**T RAINED** all week. On Sunday, as Margaret dialed
Maizon's number, her fingers trembled. The phone rang
three times before Maizon picked it up.

"He had another one," Margaret cried into the phone.
Her voice sounded tight and unfamiliar.

"Another what? Who?"

"Daddy! He had another heart attack. Mama just left.
Maizon, I'm scared."

"I'll be right over. Look out the window till I come,
okay?"

Margaret was silent. Her heart had constricted into a
tiny knot at the center of her chest.

"Okay, Margaret?" Maizon said again. She sounded
scared.

"Mama said go stay with Ms. Dell and Hattie until she

gets back," Margaret said mechanically. Everything seemed unreal, like it had happened a long time ago to somebody else.

"You can't see the bridge from Ms. Dell's window, Margaret. That's the only way not to be scared. Just watch the trains. I'll be right there. You want to talk to my grandmother until I get there?"

Margaret shook her head. She couldn't bear the calm sound of Grandma's voice right now. It would make it all too real.

"I'll go get her . . ."

"No," Margaret said quickly. "Just come, Maizon. Just you. Hurry."

Margaret hung up the phone and walked slowly over to the window. Although it was only eleven in the morning, the clouded-over sky made the day dark. The empty lot on Palmetto Street looked like a black hole big enough to swallow whole anything that came close enough. Margaret wondered when she had been this afraid.

The bridge was dimly lit and seemed to sag beneath the load of the drizzling rain. No trains were in sight. Margaret leaned against the window and thought about waking Li'l Jay.

"What if Daddy dies?" she said out loud. She saw clearly the picture on the mantelpiece behind her of her mother, father and herself before Li'l Jay was born. They were sitting beneath a tree in Prospect Park and her father had a puppet on his hand. She closed her eyes and saw her father's hand. It was big and dark and strong. There were a million wrinkles on the palm. A hand like that couldn't die, she thought. She felt it brush the hair away from her eyes. She felt his chin resting on her head, then felt a cold spot again where it had been. The chill made its way to her bones.

Margaret opened her eyes and saw Maizon's green poncho halfway down the block, then heard Ms. Dell opening the front door and Maizon's footsteps on the stairs. She waited by the door until Maizon darted in.

"You okay?" Maizon asked, pulling out of her poncho.

"Yeah . . ." Margaret's eyes were red-rimmed from crying. She wanted Maizon to hold her while she cried, but they had never done that.

"Did you hear anything from anybody?"

Margaret shook her head and sniffed. Maizon followed her to the couch. Her sneakers made squishing noises. She sat on the small patch of rug in front of the couch and began to untie them.

"They're soaking wet." She peeled off one yellow sock, then the other one, and draped them from the coffee table.

"Ms. Dell was right," Margaret said hoarsely. "She said it was going to rain hard for a long time and it's been raining for a week now." She slouched further down into the pillows. "You ever feel alone, Maizon? Like there's nobody left in the world but you that matters?"

Maizon played with the toe of one sock. "Sometimes. Sometimes I feel like I don't really matter, because if I did, my mother wouldn't have died and my daddy wouldn't have left me."

"But you have your grandmother . . . and Ms. Dell

has Hattie and Hattie has Ms. Dell and Mama has Daddy."

"You have your father and your mother and Li'l Jay. You have a whole normal family!"

"Just 'cause it's whole doesn't mean it's 'normal.' Last year we did a project in social studies on families, and my teacher said there were all kinds of families and it's not right to say only some things are normal and all other things aren't. Anyway, Daddy's sick and Mama works and Li'l Jay's too little. He can hardly talk. That leaves me. And sometimes I wish I had a grandmother all to myself or Ms. Dell all to myself or Hattie even. Just someone all to myself. I feel so stretched out. Like I'm broken in a million pieces or something."

"What about me, Margaret? You have me. We're best friends, remember?"

"You're going to go away." Tears slid down her face and Margaret wiped them away with the back of her hand. "And my daddy's going to die."

"Margaret, don't say that. Maybe I won't go away, and your daddy's not going to die."

Margaret stared at Maizon for a moment, then closed her eyes. There was too much uncertainty in Maizon's voice.

"You falling asleep?" Maizon asked.

"No."

Maizon came over and sat beside her.

"What are you doing?"

"Looking at the colors I see on the inside of my head and trying not to think of Daddy."

"What colors?"

"Grays and blues and greens."

Maizon leaned back and closed her eyes.

"I see yellows and browns and reds. It looks like the fall. Since we're special, we probably see colors no one else in the whole world sees."

"Uh huh," Margaret said.

"Margaret? I'm starting to see some blues too."

Best friends should always see the same things, Margaret thought, reaching for Maizon's hand. For a long time they sat in silence. Margaret heard Maizon snoring softly beside her. In a little while, she, too, dozed off.

When Ms. Tory walked in late in the afternoon, they jumped. Her face was ashen and streaked with rain. Her eyes, slanted like Margaret's, were now puffy and swollen. Margaret's eyes rested on her mother's mouth. It was pulled into a tight, solemn line and for a moment she thought her mother was angry, but then she realized it was something worse than anger. Much, much worse. Li'l Jay began to cry in the next room and Maizon left to quiet him.

"How's Daddy?" Margaret asked, afraid to look at her mother's eyes. If she did, she knew she would see that the worst was happening.

Ms. Tory sank to the couch and pulled Margaret to her. She held her tightly and cried into Margaret's shoulder. "I tried to call you, sweetheart. I wanted you to see him before . . ."

Margaret knew then that her father would not be home again. A lump rose in her own throat. Tears pushed against the insides of her eyes. "No, Mama," she whispered.

"I wanted you to see him before he died, Margaret. But when they pressed that . . . that mask against his face I knew it was too late."

"Please, Mama," Margaret begged, holding on to her mother's sleeves. "Tell me he didn't die, Mama, please!"

"I don't know what's going to happen to us now, Margaret. I just don't know."

Margaret felt her father's hands on her shoulders. A warm breath brushed against her forehead. She swallowed. "We're going to be okay, Mama," she whispered. Her voice was small and uncertain. "I promise, Mama. We're going to be okay."

CHAPTER 5

W HEN MARGARET walked into Li'l Jay's room, the rain was beating out a soft one-two against the pane. Night was coming on quickly and thunder cracked across the sky. Maizon was sitting on the floor beside Li'l Jay's crib. Margaret tiptoed over and kneeled beside her.

"I should go home, I guess," Maizon said, starting to rise. She had been crying.

"My daddy died today," Margaret whispered. She opened her mouth and closed it, then turned to Maizon and tried to speak again. "Died," she said, and in the crazy night air of the rainstorm, the word had a strange echo to it. She stared into Li'l Jay's crib. His thumb crept slowly to his mouth and soft sucking sounds mingled with storm.

She pressed her face against his crib. "Daddy died today," she said again. "He's not coming home."

Margaret knew she was trying to make sense of the words, rolling them around on her tongue until they found a place to settle in her brain; a place where they'd become real.

"Margaret," Maizon whispered, "my grandmother said when people go to heaven, there's a rainbow when they smile."

Margaret stared at her as though she were just realizing Maizon was in the room. She got up and walked slowly over to the window.

"You see anything, Margaret?"

"No, nothing. Not even a little blue," Margaret said.

"It's too dark out," Maizon whispered.

"Maybe he's not smiling, Maizon. Maybe it still hurts."

"Maybe he hasn't gotten there yet. Heaven's a long way away."

"You think so?"

"He'll be there tomorrow," Maizon said.

They stared out into the darkness.

"I don't know what's going to happen now, Maizon. I bet even Ms. Dell doesn't know. We might move away."

"You can't move away, Margaret! Best friends don't move away from each other," Maizon cried.

"Ms. Dell says they do sometimes, remember?"

"Ms. Dell doesn't know *everything*, Margaret."

"She knows a lot, though," Margaret said, walking slowly back over to Li'l Jay's crib. "Sometimes I wish she didn't know so much."

The rain had dropped to a whisper against the window. They watched the drops trickle down the pane slowly, branching out in every direction before hitting the bottom.

Margaret brushed the cookie crumbs from Li'l Jay's lips and stared down at him. Li'l Jay twitched in his sleep and sighed.

"He's lucky," Maizon said. "He doesn't even understand anything yet."

Margaret bent over and kissed Li'l Jay. "No, he's not, Maizon. He won't know anything about my father except the things I tell him. I'm the lucky one, I guess. At least I knew him."

Maizon followed her out of the room.

Margaret's mother lay on the couch with her hand covering her eyes. She sat up when they walked in and ran her fingers through her hair.

"I called your grandmother, Maizon. She said it was okay for you to stay here tonight."

"Thank you, Ms. Tory," Maizon said, staring at her toes.

"Mama, you want some tea?"

"No, thank you, dear. I'm going out again."

Ms. Tory went into the hallway and began pulling on her rain boots. Margaret and Maizon followed her. The boots were still wet from her last trip.

"I have to go to the funeral home. Hattie's going to come with me. Ms. Dell said she'd come up if you want her to. She said you and Maizon might want to be alone a while. Will you be okay?"

Margaret was frantic. "Can I go with you, Mama? Please! Maizon can stay with Li'l Jay. Please, Mama!"

Ms. Tory looked from Margaret to Maizon.

"I think it's best if you stay here, dear," she said softly.

"But you'll get sick in the rain, Mama! You'll get sick like Daddy," Margaret cried.

Ms. Tory pulled Margaret to her. Maizon looked on, twisting her hands.

"No, no, no, Margaret," she said softly. "I'll be fine. If it gets too late, we'll take a taxi. Don't worry, sweetheart." She kissed Margaret's forehead.

"Mama . . . ?" Margaret whispered.

Ms. Tory held her, blinking back tears.

"Please come back, Mama."

Ms. Tory held her for a long time. "I'll always come back, Margaret. Always."

They followed her into the baby's room and waited while Ms. Tory leaned over the crib and kissed Li'l Jay. Then she kissed them both again and left. Margaret bolted each lock after her mother was gone. They trailed into Margaret's room and plopped down onto the bed. Maizon brought out her hair pick.

"Want to comb my hair, Margaret?"

Margaret nodded. Something about combing Maizon's hair always made her feel better.

Maizon sat on the bed and handed Margaret the pick. Margaret kneeled on the bed above Maizon's head. She pulled the pick gently through the thick, wiry hair.

"I sure wish I had an Afro."

"I wish my hair was long like yours. Then I'd put it in cornrows and everything. I'd wear curls for picture day."

After a moment Maizon said, "Margaret, do you think Ms. Dell knew about your daddy?"

"Maybe she knew more than me," Margaret said softly, quickly brushing away a tear that was sliding toward her mouth, "because she and Mama talked about Daddy being sick and everything."

"Death is mean. Isn't it, Margaret? He takes and takes and takes. First he took Hattie's baby. Just up and took it right out from under all those breathing tubes they had strapped to that poor baby."

"I hate death. I hate it that my daddy's not coming home again!"

"My daddy never came home again," Maizon said quietly.

"But your daddy didn't die. He just went away," Margaret said, lowering her voice.

"He might as well be dead," Maizon said, lying back on the bed. Margaret knew Maizon's father had left her with her grandmother when she was a baby, right after her mother died. Maizon had never known either of them but she had often wondered where her father was. She had not talked about him in a long time.

"At least there's a chance he might come back, Maizon. My daddy's never coming back."

Tears rolled down the side of Maizon's face, collecting in her ears. Margaret cried too.

"Even if he does come back, Margaret," Maizon said, "I'll treat him like he never even lived!"

"Don't let them take the life out of you, Daddy," Margaret said silently. She saw him standing before her.

"What's makes you think your daddy's gonna let something like that happen? It would take a lot for one of them skinny plastic tubes to bring this six-footer down."

Margaret heard her father laugh. The laughter sounded far away.

"Margaret, are you listening to me?" Maizon nearly shouted. She jerked her head toward Margaret, then moved closer.

"What did they do with my daddy?" Margaret whispered. She pushed her fist into her mouth to keep from screaming.

"Margaret!" Maizon shouted. "Don't, Margaret, you're scaring me!"

Margaret bounded off the bed and ran over to the window. "Where is my daddy?" she shouted into the storm, then crumpled to the floor. "Where is he, Maizon? Where'd they take my daddy to?" Her voice was ragged and tired.

Maizon trembled as she walked toward Margaret. "He's in heaven," she said, kneeling down beside her. Her hand felt soft and warm on Margaret's shoulder. Maizon leaned against the wall and Margaret rested her head on Maizon's chest. She could hear Maizon's heartbeat beneath the thin cotton shirt. The sound was soothing, very soothing.

"Why'd he have to die, Maizon?" she whispered. Maizon wrapped her arms around her and began rocking slowly back and forth.

"Maybe heaven needs him now," Maizon said. She began to sing. The song was about a place in heaven where good people have to go. It was about babies and mothers and old men. The lyrics brought fresh tears to Margaret's eyes. She cried long and hard, but Maizon held on.

❧ CHAPTER 6 ❧

T HE FUNERAL had been long and hot. Now Margaret and Maizon sat on the curb in front of Margaret's building in matching black dresses and etched their names into the tar. Maizon dug a hole in the street over the *i* and Margaret wished for a moment that there were an *i* in her name so that she could do the same.

In the distance they heard the sound of construction. A crew had started working on the lot on Palmetto Street.

Margaret dropped the sharpened Popsicle stick she had been digging with and put her hands over her ears. Everything reminded her of death: the construction, the sticky black tar, the heat, their black dresses.

A street cleaner made its way slowly down the street and they watched the truck sweep the discarded cans and paper bags away from the curb. Maizon held her nose as the spray of bleach-scented water wafted toward them.

"That street cleaner seems to be coming around more and more," Margaret said, watching the truck disappear down the block.

"That's because of the construction. Ms. Dell says rich people are going to move into those new buildings and if rich people want clean streets," Maizon turned to Margaret and grimaced, "then rich people get clean streets."

"Hattie says that's going to be a grocery store," Margaret said skeptically.

"Then it's going to be a grocery store for rich people who want clean streets," Maizon said, concentrating again on her *i*.

Margaret looked up at her window. People had been upstairs for hours eating and laughing and talking about what a good man her father had been. She wanted to take a nap. But there were even people in her bedroom!

"Maizon, let's go to your house."

"Why?" Maizon frowned. "All the good food is in your house."

"But there are too many people there, and I'm tired."

Maizon looked puzzled for a moment, then agreed. "Me too," she said. "It's too hot out here, anyway."

They walked down the quiet block, past the one tree on Madison Street. Margaret stopped.

"Maizon, remember when we were little and we couldn't go past this tree? So we'd meet here."

"And then I decided to call it the compromise spot," Maizon said proudly.

40

"Because it's the same distance from both our houses."
Margaret smiled, looking at the tree as though she were
seeing it for the first time. "That seems like forever ago."

"Yeah." Maizon moved closer to the tree. "Hey, Margaret, check this out," she said, pointing to the spot on the
tree where she and Margaret had dug a hole and stuck a
branch in, two years before. "The branch is gone."

Margaret peered into the hole.

"Maybe a bird used it for her nest."

"Yeah," Maizon said. "Maybe."

They continued down the street. Maizon undid the
latch on the heavy black gate in front of her house and
rang the bell.

"Maizon, use those keys!" her grandmother called
from inside.

Maizon pulled two silver keys out of her sock and
smiled at Margaret. She unlocked the two locks on the
walnut-brown door. It creaked open with a whine. Margaret followed her into the cool, dimly lit vestibule that
led to the kitchen.

Maizon's grandmother stood at the counter, her back
to them. Margaret grabbed Maizon's hand and put a finger to her lips. "I want to watch her for a moment," she
whispered.

Maizon's grandmother's skin was warmed with gold.
"She's Cheyenne Indian," Maizon had bragged. "That
makes me an Indian princess, almost." Her silver hair
was French braided and pinned at the nape of her neck.
Her shoulders shook as she sprinkled cinnamon onto

rolls, and she was humming softly. She stopped suddenly.

"Don't I get a greeting or a kiss? You two act like spies, coming into my kitchen not saying anything." She turned and flashed a smile. Her teeth were small and even. Maizon had said they were false but Margaret didn't care. The smile was real.

"Hi, Grandma," Margaret said.

"Margaret wanted to watch you," Maizon tattled.

Margaret followed Maizon over and waited her turn for one of Grandma's kisses. She loved kissing Maizon's grandmother because she always held you tightly afterward like it had been ages since she'd last seen you and ages before she'd see you again.

"You seem to be getting along just fine, Margaret. I am so sorry about your daddy," Maizon's grandmother said, holding Margaret. "Oh, but the funeral was beautiful, wasn't it? Just beautiful. I sure will miss him."

"Margaret just wishes everyone would leave her house already!" Maizon said, going over to the refrigerator and looking for something to drink.

Grandma turned around and frowned at Maizon. "Cat got Margaret's tongue? Let her do her own talking. Put those rolls in the oven for me."

"Yes, ma'am!" Maizon saluted her grandmother.

"If your mother wasn't having such a hard time, I'd ask her to trade kids with me. This one here is just too smart for her own good!"

They laughed.

"So how long has it been, Margaret, since your daddy passed away?"

"Four days," Margaret said quietly, feeling her throat close around the words. She took a seat in the wooden rocking chair.

"I know it seems like a lot longer than that, doesn't it?" Grandma said.

"Uh huh."

"Girl, the Lord works his magic in ways we don't understand. You wonder who He is and why He does what He does. But you know it's not for us to question."

"Uh huh," Margaret said, feeling sleepy and safe in the cinnamon-scented kitchen. The smoothness of Grandma's voice floated over and comforted her. She didn't want Grandma to stop speaking.

"When I was a little girl on the reservation I came home one day to find my father had died. I didn't want to believe it because my father had always been there to help me with what I was doing. We'd make shoes out of animal skins and hunt birds and sow corn and laugh with each other. But then . . . he wasn't coming home anymore. The Cheyenne Indians have a custom—to take a part of something that belonged to the person who has died and bury it with that person. I took the last thing we had made together, a feather cape for the games I played, and buried it next to my father. I wanted him to know a part of me would always be with him the way a part of him would be with me. And you know something, I believe he went to heaven knowing that." Grandma smiled at Margaret.

"Grandma," Maizon said from the refrigerator, "we don't have any punch."

"If you're old enough to realize that, you're old enough to make some. Now, you know where the mix is and you know where the water is."

Margaret sat up in the chair. She loved reservation stories.

"My granddaughter may be smart, but she doesn't always have what is most important—common sense. Margaret, you have common sense. You know you are tired now and would like to take a nap. So why don't you go on up to Maizon's room and lie down? I'll wake you when the rolls are ready."

"Hey, what about the punch I'm making?" Maizon said from the sink.

"I'll drink it when I wake up," Margaret promised, heading toward the stairs.

Maizon sucked her teeth. "Sleepyhead," she mumbled.

Maizon's grandmother put her hand on Maizon's shoulder and said, "Let her rest, Maiz."

Margaret made her way down the quiet hallway. The stairs were covered with the same brown carpet as the living room, but the upstairs floors were bare. This part of Maizon's house always smelled like wax and wood. Over the years, Margaret had come to love that smell.

Maizon's room was pink, with rainbow sheets and a matching comforter. She had shelves of books and stuffed animals. The dark oak dresser matched the wood of her canopied bed. Margaret wondered why Maizon loved sleeping at her house so much when she had such a great room. But she was too sleepy to think about it now.

She took off her black patent leather shoes and climbed up onto Maizon's bed. She watched the sun stream through the curtains for a while. Thoughts of her father brought fresh tears to her eyes. They had never made things the way Grandma did but they had talked about things. And he would sing to her. Margaret thought about the song he used to sing about blue skies after rainstorms and someone watching over her. Grandma's voice drifted up from the kitchen.

"You have to be patient with Margaret, Maizon," Grandma was saying. "Death is hard. You're lucky you haven't experienced it."

"My mama died. Then Daddy went away. And I knew Mr. Tory."

"It's not the same," Grandma said patiently. "Your mama died when you were just a baby and your father left when you were not much older than that. You knew neither of them. And Mr. Tory you didn't know much better. He was just your friend and not a very close one. But he was Margaret's father. A father she had known."

"Margaret seems sadder now, Grandma," Maizon said.

"And she will be for a long time. Just be patient with her, Maizon. And be a friend."

"I am her friend, Grandma. We're best friends!"

"Sometimes being a friend is harder than you think, Maizon. My people had a saying for that, you know. They said a friend is someone who knows when to be there and when not to be."

"Friends should always be together, Grandma."

"Not always, Maizon. Not always," Grandma said. Their voices were coming from the living room now. Margaret wondered if this was eavesdropping. She closed her eyes and tried to shut the voices out. She heard the knitting needles clicking softly and imagined Grandma's hands moving swiftly over the dark-green yarn she was working with these days.

"I had a friend, Maizon," she heard Grandma say softly. The knitting needles were silent, which meant Grandma was leaning toward Maizon, about to tell an important story. *Grandma loves sharing stories, so it couldn't be eavesdropping,* Margaret thought. ". . . before I married your grandfather. I thought I knew her so well and she knew me even better. We grew up together in Colorado. She, too, lived on the reservation before the government came and took us from the land. But I brought your grandfather to meet her and she said to me, 'You can't marry him. He's a black man.' I knew that there had come a point where I still called this girl my friend but we didn't even know each other. Because I loved your grandfather and saw him as someone I loved. But she saw him as black and refused to know him."

"But Margaret and I agree on everything."

"You won't always, though. If the Lord separates you from her and you go to that school, you will learn things that are different from what Margaret is learning. You will grow in different ways."

"Then I don't want to go away."

And I don't want you to go away, Margaret thought.

"But, Maizon, you must understand, you have to grow. I remembered my childhood with this friend and I kept those memories because they were important to me. But I knew she had grown into someone I wasn't. I still love her for who she was, not who she became. Do you understand, Maizon?"

"No," Maizon said stubbornly.

"Oh, but you will. You will."

Margaret fell asleep to the soft clicking of Grandma's needles.

⫷C H A P T E R   7⫸

WHEN nearly another month passed with no word from Blue Hill, Margaret let her hopes rise a little. Saturday was sunny and hot, a perfect day for a block party. Madison Street was noisy and filled with kids, happy that the street was closed off to traffic. From the kitchen, Margaret heard Maizon bound up the stairs and pound on the door. Ms. Tory sat in the living room with Li'l Jay on her lap, gazing absently out the window. Margaret heard Li'l Jay yell when Maizon entered.

"Hi, Ms. Tory! Your door's unlocked. Where's Margaret?" she shouted.

"She's in the kitchen helping me get this baby something to eat. I see you're all ready for the block party. What do you have there?" she asked.

"Something I gotta tell Margaret about right away!"

Maizon darted into the kitchen just as Margaret pulled Li'l Jay's bottle from the pan of hot water.

"Hey, Maizon! When I finish with this bottle we can practice our double-dutch again before the contest. Did you bring the rope?"

Maizon gasped. "I forgot."

"Maizon, how could you forget? We've been practicing for a week now."

"I got into Blue Hill!" Maizon shouted, handing Margaret a white envelope.

Margaret ripped the letter from it and moved her lips silently as she read.

"Maizon! They want you to leave September first! That's not even two weeks away!"

"I know, and I still have to pack and buy clothes and say goodbye and . . ."

"But, Maizon, you're leaving in two weeks! Two weeks! Don't you care!"

"About what?"

"About leaving," Margaret said, carrying the bottle into the living room. Her hand shook as she handed it to her mother.

"Maizon got into Blue Hill, Mama," she said, inching off to her room. Behind her she heard her mother congratulating Maizon.

"Yeah, wonderful," Margaret whispered, flinging the window open.

She stared out at the construction site. The usually noisy cranes and trucks were still. The frame of the building was complete now, four stories higher than her own. Margaret sighed. She felt so empty all of a sudden.

"You sad 'cause I'm going away, Margaret?" Maizon asked from the doorway.

"I don't care," Margaret said.

"I wish you were going, too, Margaret. I didn't even think of us not being together when I first got the letter. All I thought about was how happy my grandmother was. She said this was a good chance for me to meet different kinds of people and get a real good education."

"But there are different kinds of people here, Maizon. And more people are going to move in. Rich people."

"I know. But I know just about everyone here and P.S. 102 doesn't have such good teachers. Remember last year when I knew more than Ms. Shawn?"

Margaret frowned and nodded.

"Blue Hill is supposed to be smarter than any school in Brooklyn. And since I got a scholarship, my grandmother says I should go. She says I could get into good colleges and everything!"

"College?"

Maizon came over to the window.

"I know it's a long way away. But my grandmother says I should start thinking."

After a moment Margaret asked, "What's Blue Hill going to be like?"

"I don't know. Lots of strangers dressed alike. Scary. I heard there are hardly any black people there. I won't know anybody."

"Maizon, I don't want you to go away." Margaret

pressed her face against the cool pane. She didn't feel like double-dutch or block parties or anything anymore. "I was wishing you wouldn't get accepted."

"I was hoping that too," Maizon said. "But now that I got in, I know I have to go."

"Yeah, I guess so," Margaret sighed. "I guess everyone has to go away sometime."

"We can still buy the same clothes, Margaret. The letter says we don't have to wear uniforms until the second week."

Margaret nodded. What did it matter? They were going to be wearing them so far away from each other.

"Maizon, you think Ms. Dell was right about us? Remember she said one day all the things we did together won't matter 'cause other things will be more important?"

"Ah, I don't believe that, Margaret! I know you'll always be my best friend and I'll always be yours. It'll still be just like we're living on the same block."

"You think so? You think we'll still be best friends? Connecticut is a long way away."

"If we promise to be."

"I promise. I promise I won't talk to anybody about any secrets but you. Sometimes I'll talk to Hattie and Ms. Dell, and Mama . . . and maybe Li'l Jay, when he can carry on a conversation."

"And I'll only talk to teachers. I'll write you about everything and call you and tell you what happens every day."

They were silent for a long moment. Slowly, Margaret

began to realize Maizon was really going away. The thought was a dull ache that started at her feet and worked its way up to her heart. She groped for words to fill the silence, but found none.

"Maybe I can visit, Maizon," she said weakly.

"Yeah, and maybe I can come home on the weekend sometimes!"

"And maybe I can get a scholarship if I study and get real smart like you!"

"Yeah!"

"Promise always, Maizon?"

"Uh huh. You promise?"

"Uh huh."

Maizon leaned over and kissed her gently on the cheek. Margaret was startled. She put her hand to her cheek and looked at Maizon.

"You're my best friend in the whole world," Maizon said solemnly. "I love you. Best friends should tell each other that."

"You're mine, too, Maizon," Margaret said softly, still a little surprised.

"And . . . ?" Maizon prodded.

"And I love you." Margaret smiled.

"Come on then," Maizon said, sounding slightly embarrassed. "We have a double-dutch contest!"

They raced past Ms. Tory and Li'l Jay and slammed out the front door.

"Hey! Hey! Where you two off to so fast?" Ms. Dell said. She and Hattie were sitting on the stoop. They had done most of the baking for the block party and now glanced proudly at the table in front of them. "Come back here and try one of these desserts me and Hattie put so much time into," Ms. Dell said, fanning herself with her hand.

Maizon inched backward toward a strawberry-frosted cake with white sugar roses. She scooped up a fingerful from behind her back and turned quickly to stuff the frosting into her mouth.

"I guess you think no one saw that, Maizon?" Ms. Dell teased, folding her arms across her chest.

"We have to go," Maizon said quickly, grabbing Margaret's hand. "It's almost time for the contest."

She pulled Margaret behind her.

Maizon began chanting what they had practiced. "Almost twins. We're best friends, jumpin' side by side." Margaret joined in.

"Turn around, touch the ground, up and give me five." They slapped their palms together.

"Almost twins—could be cousins—coolest girls alive!" They sang as they made their way toward the crowd of girls that had gathered for the contest.

≈ CHAPTER 8 ≈

"**S**URE WISH you weren't going away," Margaret said, choking back tears for what seemed like the millionth time. They were sitting on the M train, crossing the Williamsburg Bridge, and Margaret shivered as the train passed over the water. The L train would have made the trip easier but the L didn't go over the bridge and Maizon had wanted to ride over it once more before she left.

Maizon sat nervously drumming her fingers against the windowpane. "Me too," she said absently.

Margaret looked over at Mama and Grandma. Grandma stared out of her window. She looked old and out of place on the train.

"Maizon?" Margaret said, turning back toward her.

"Hmm?" Maizon frowned. She seemed to be concentrating on something in the water. It rippled and danced below them.

"Even though I wrote you those two letters, you only have to write me one back if you don't have a lot of time or something." Margaret looked down at her fingers. She had begun biting the cuticles, and now the skin surrounding her nails was red and ragged.

"I'll write you back," Maizon promised.

"Maizon . . ."

"What, Margaret!"

Margaret jumped and looked at Maizon. There was an uneasiness in her eyes she had never seen before.

"Forget it," she said.

Ms. Tory leaned over. "We'll be getting off in a few stops."

They rode the rest of the way in silence. At Delancey Street they changed for another train and a half hour later they were at Penn Station.

"I guess now we'll have to call each other to plan the same outfits," Maizon said as they waited for her train. Her voice sounded forced and fake, Margaret thought, like a grown-up trying to make a kid smile.

"I guess," Margaret said. The conductor called Maizon's train.

"I guess I gotta go," Maizon said softly, and Margaret felt a lump rise in her throat.

"I'll write you back, Margaret. Promise. Thanks for letting me keep the double-dutch trophy even if it is only second place." They hugged for a long time. Maizon sniffed loudly. "I'm scared, Margaret," she whispered.

Margaret didn't know what to say. "Don't be."

"Bye, Ms. Tory."

Margaret's mother bent down and hugged Maizon. "Be good," she said as Maizon and her grandmother made their way toward the train.

"Mama," Margaret said as they watched Maizon and her grandmother disappear into the tunnel.

"What, dear?"

"What's the difference between a best friend and an old friend?"

"I guess . . ." Her mother thought for a moment. "I guess an old friend is a friend you once had and a best friend is a friend you'll always have."

"Then maybe me and Maizon aren't best friends anymore."

"Don't be silly, Margaret. What else would you two be? Some people can barely tell you apart. I feel like I've lost a daughter."

"Maybe . . . I don't know . . . Maybe we're old friends now. Maybe this was our last summer as best friends. I feel like something's going to change now and I'm not going to be able to change it back."

Ms. Tory's heels made a clicking sound through the terminal. She stopped to buy tokens and turned to Margaret.

"Like when Daddy died?" she asked, looking worried.

Margaret swallowed. "No. I just feel empty instead of sad, Mama," she said.

Her mother squeezed her hand as they waited for the train. When it came, they took seats by the window.

Ms. Tory held on to Margaret's hand. "Sometimes it just takes a while for the pain of loss to set in."

"I feel like sometimes Maizon kept me from doing things, but now she's not here. Now I don't have any"— Margaret thought for a moment, but couldn't find the right words—"now I don't have any excuse not to do things."

When the train emerged from its tunnel, the late afternoon sun had turned a bright orange. Margaret watched it for a moment. She looked at her hands again and discovered a cuticle she had missed.

CHAPTER 9

MARGARET pressed her pencil to her lips and stared out the classroom window. The school yard was desolate and gray. But everything seemed that way since Maizon left. Especially since a whole week had passed now without even a letter from her. Margaret sighed and chewed her eraser.

"Margaret, are you working on this assignment?"

Margaret jumped and turned toward Ms. Peazle. Maizon had been right—Ms. Peazle was the crabbiest teacher in the school. Margaret wondered why she had been picked to teach the smartest class. If students were so smart, she thought, the least the school could do was reward them with a nice teacher.

"I'm trying to think about what to write, Ms. Peazle."

"Well, you won't find an essay on your summer vacation outside that window, I'm sure. Or is that where you spent it?"

The class snickered and Margaret looked down, embarrassed. "No, ma'am."

"I'm glad to hear that," Ms. Peazle continued, looking at Margaret over granny glasses. "And I'm sure in the next ten minutes you'll be able to read your essay to the class and prove to us all that you weren't just daydreaming. Am I right?"

"I hope so, ma'am," Margaret mumbled. She looked around the room. It seemed everyone in 6–1 knew each other from the previous year. On the first day, a lot of kids asked her about Maizon, but after that no one said much to her. Things had changed since Maizon left. Without her, a lot of the fun had gone out of sitting on the stoop with Ms. Dell, Hattie, and Li'l Jay. Maybe she could write about that. No, Margaret thought, looking down at the blank piece of paper in front of her. It was too much to tell. She'd never get finished and Ms. Peazle would scold her—making her feel too dumb to be in 6–1. Margaret chewed her eraser and stared out the window again. There had to be something she could write about quickly.

"Margaret Tory!" Ms. Peazle warned. "Am I going to have to change your seat?"

"Ma'am? I was just . . ."

"I think I'm going to have to move you away from that window unless you can prove to me that you can sit there without being distracted."

"I can, Ms. Peazle. It helps me write," she lied.

"Then I take it you should be ready to read your essay in"—Ms. Peazle looked at her watch—"the next seven minutes."

Margaret started writing frantically. When Ms. Peazle called her to the front of the room, her sheet of notebook paper shook in her hand. She pulled nervously at the hem of the maroon dress she and Maizon had picked out for school and tried not to look out at the twenty-six pairs of eyes she knew were on her.

"Last summer was the worst summer of my life. First my father died and then my best friend went away to a private boarding school. I didn't go anywhere except Manhattan. But that wasn't any fun because I was taking Maizon to the train. I hope next summer is a lot better."

She finished reading and walked silently back to her desk and tried to concentrate on not looking out the window. Instead, she rested her eyes on the half-written page. Margaret knew she could write better than that, but Ms. Peazle had rushed her. Anyway, she thought, that *is* what happened last summer.

"I'd like to see you after class, Margaret."

"Yes, ma'am," Margaret said softly. *This is the end,* she thought. One week in the smartest class and it's over. Maizon was smart enough to go to a better *school* and I can't even keep up in this class. Margaret sighed and tried not to stare out the window for the rest of the day.

When the three o'clock bell rang, she waited uneasily in her seat while Ms. Peazle led the rest of the class out to the school yard. Margaret heard the excited screams and laughter as everyone poured outside.

The empty classroom was quiet. She looked around at the desks. Many had words carved into them. They reminded her of the names she and Maizon had carved into the tar last summer. They were faded and illegible now.

Ms. Peazle came in and sat at the desk next to Margaret's. "Margaret," she said slowly, pausing for a moment to remove her glasses and rub her eyes tiredly. "I'm sorry to hear about your father . . ."

"That's okay." Margaret fidgeted.

"No, Margaret, it's not okay," Ms. Peazle continued, "not if it's going to affect your schoolwork."

"I can do better, Ms. Peazle, I really can!" Margaret looked up pleadingly. She was surprised at herself for wanting so badly to stay in Ms. Peazle's class.

"I know you can, Margaret. That's why I'm going to ask you to do this. For homework tonight . . ."

Margaret started to say that none of the other students had been assigned homework. She decided not to, though.

"I want you to write about your summer," Ms. Peazle continued. "I want it to express all of your feelings about your friend Maizon going away. Or it could be about your father's death and how you felt then. It doesn't matter what you write, a poem, an essay, a short story. Just so long as it expresses how you felt this summer. Is that understood?"

"Yes, ma'am." Margaret looked up at Ms. Peazle. "It's understood."

Ms. Peazle smiled. Without her glasses, Margaret thought, she wasn't that mean-looking.

"Good, then I'll see you bright and early tomorrow
with something wonderful to read to the class."

Margaret slid out of the chair and walked toward the
door.

"That's a very pretty dress, Margaret," Ms. Peazle said.

Margaret turned and started to tell her that Maizon was
wearing the same one in Connecticut, but changed her
mind. What did Ms. Peazle know about best friends who
were almost cousins, anyway?

"Thanks, ma'am," she said instead, and ducked out of
the classroom. All of a sudden, she had a wonderful idea!

❧ CHAPTER 10 ❧

THE NEXT morning Ms. Peazle tapped her ruler against the desk to quiet the class. "Margaret," she asked when the room was silent. "Do you have something you want to share with us today?"

Margaret nodded and Ms. Peazle beckoned her to the front of the room.

"This," Margaret said, handing Ms. Peazle the sheet of looseleaf paper. It had taken her most of the evening to finish the assignment.

Ms. Peazle looked it over and handed it back to her.

"We're ready to listen," she said, smiling.

Margaret looked out over the class and felt her stomach slide up to her throat. She swallowed and counted to ten. Though the day was cool, she found herself sweating.

Margaret couldn't remember when she had been this afraid.

"My pen doesn't write anymore," she began reading.

"I can't hear," someone called out.

"My pen doesn't write anymore," Margaret repeated. In the back of the room, someone exaggerated a sigh. The class chuckled. Margaret ignored them and continued to read.

"It stumbles and trembles in my hand.
If my dad were here—he would understand.
Best of all—It'd be last summer again.

But they've turned off the fire hydrants
Locked green leaves away.
Sprinkled ashes on you
and sent you on your way.

I wouldn't mind the early autumn
if you came home today
I'd tell you how much I miss you
and know I'd be okay.

Mama isn't laughing now
She works hard and she cries
she wonders when true laughter
will relieve her of her sighs
And even when she's smiling
Her eyes don't smile along
her face is growing older

She doesn't seem as strong.
I worry cause I love her
Ms. Dell says, 'where there is love,
there is a way.'

It's funny how we never know
exactly how our life will go
It's funny how a dream can fade
With the break of day.

I'm not sure where you are now
though I see you in my dreams
Ms. Dell says the things we see
are not always as they seem.

So often I'm uncertain
if you have found a new home
and when I am uncertain
I usually write a poem.

Time can't erase the memory
and time can't bring you home
Last summer was a part of me
and now a part is gone."

The class stared at her blankly, silent. Margaret lowered her head and made her way back to her seat.

"Could you leave that assignment on my desk, Margaret?" Ms. Peazle asked. There was a small smile playing at the corners of her mouth.

"Yes, ma'am," Margaret said. Why didn't anyone say anything?

"Now, if everyone will open their history books to page two seventy-five, we'll continue with our lesson on the Civil War."

Margaret wondered what she had expected the class to do. Applaud? She missed Maizon more than she had in a long time. *She would know what I'm feeling,* Margaret thought. And if she didn't, she'd make believe she did.

Margaret snuck a look out the window. The day looked cold and still. *She'd tell me it's only a feeling poets get and that Nikki Giovanni feels this way all of the time.* When she turned back, there was a small piece of paper on her desk.

"I liked your poem, Margaret," the note read. There was no name.

Margaret looked around but no one looked as though they had slipped a note on her desk. She smiled to herself and tucked the piece of paper into her notebook.

The final bell rang. As the class rushed out, Margaret was bumped against Ms. Peazle's desk.

"Did you get my note?" Ms. Peazle whispered. Margaret nodded and floated home.

Ms. Dell, Hattie, and Li'l Jay were sitting on the stoop when she got home.

"If it weren't so cold," she said, squeezing in beside Hattie's spreading hips, "it would be like old times."

"Except for Maizon," Hattie said, cutting her eyes toward her mother.

"Hush, Hattie," Ms. Dell said. She shivered and pulled

Li'l Jay closer to her. For a moment, Margaret thought she looked old.

"It's just this cold spell we're having," Ms. Dell said. "Ages a person. Makes them look older than they are."

Margaret smiled. "Reading minds is worse than eavesdropping, Ms. Dell."

"Try being her daughter for nineteen years," Hattie said.

"Hattie," Margaret said, moving closer to her for warmth. "How come you never liked Maizon?"

"No one said I never liked her."

"No one had to," Ms. Dell butted in.

"She was just too much ahead of everyone. At least she thought she was."

"But she was, Hattie. She was the smartest person at P.S. 102. Imagine being the smartest person."

"But she didn't have any common sense, Margaret. And when God gives a person that much brain, he's bound to leave out something else."

"Like what?"

Ms. Dell leaned over Li'l Jay's head and whispered loudly, "Like the truth."

She and Hattie laughed but Margaret couldn't see the humor. It wasn't like either of them to say something wrong about a person.

"She told the truth . . ." Margaret said weakly.

Ms. Dell and Hattie exchanged looks.

"How was school?" Hattie asked too brightly.

"Boring," Margaret said. She would tuck what they said away until she could figure it out.

"That's the only word you know since Maizon left. Seems there's gotta be somethin' else going on that's not so *boring* all the time," Ms. Dell said.

"Well, it's sure not school. I read a poem to that stupid class and no one but Ms. Peazle liked it." She sighed and rested her chin on her hand.

"That's the chance you gotta take with poetry," Ms. Dell said. "Either everybody likes it or everybody hates it, but you hardly ever know 'cause nobody says a word. Too afraid to offend you or, worse yet, make you feel good."

Margaret looked from Ms. Dell to Hattie then back to Ms. Dell again.

"How come you know so much about poetry?"

"You're not the first li'l black girl who wanted to be a poet."

"And you can bet your dress you won't be the last," Hattie concluded.

"You wanted to be a poet, Hattie??!!"

"Still do. Still make up poems in my head. Never write them down, though. The paper just yellows and clutters useful places. So this is where I keep it all now," she said, pointing to her head.

"A poem can't exist inside your head. You forget it," Margaret said doubtfully.

"Poems don't exist, Miss Know-It-All. Poems live! In your head is where a poem is born, isn't it?"

Margaret nodded and Hattie continued. "Well, my poetry chooses to live there!"

"Then recite one for me, please." Margaret folded her

arms across her chest the way she had seen Ms. Dell do so many times.

"Some poems aren't meant to be heard, smarty-pants."

"Aw, Hattie," Ms. Dell interrupted, "let Margaret be the judge of that."

"All right. All right." Hattie's voice dropped to a whisper. "Brooklyn-bound robin redbreast followed me from down home / Brooklyn-bound robin, you're a long way from your own / So fly among the pigeons and circle the sky with your song."

They were quiet. Ms. Dell rocked Li'l Jay to sleep in her arms. Hattie looked somberly over the block in silence and Margaret thought of how much Hattie's poem made her think of Maizon. What was she doing now that the sun was almost down? she wondered. Had she found a new best friend?

"Maybe," she said after a long time. "Maybe it wasn't that the class didn't like my poem. Maybe it was like your poem, Hattie. You just have to sit quietly and think about all the things it makes you think about after you hear it. You have to let . . . let it sink in!"

"You have to feel it, Margaret," Hattie said softly, draping her arm over Margaret's shoulder.

"Yeah. Just like I felt when I wrote my poem, or you felt when you found a place for that one in your head!"

"Margaret," Ms. Dell said, "you gettin' too smart for us ol' ladies."

Margaret leaned against Hattie and listened to the fading sounds of construction. Soon the building on Palmetto Street would be finished. She closed her eyes and visions of last summer came into her head. She saw her-self running down Madison Street arm in arm with Maizon. They were laughing. Then the picture faded into a new one. She and Maizon were sitting by the tree watching Li'l Jay take his first steps. He stumbled and fell into Maizon's arms. Now it all seemed like such a long time ago.

When she opened her eyes again, the moon was inch-ing out from behind a cloud. It was barely visible in the late afternoon. The sky had turned a wintry blue and the streetlights flickered on. Margaret yawned, her head heavy all of a sudden from the long day.

"Looks like your mother's workin' late again. Bless that woman's heart. Seems she's workin' nonstop since your daddy passed."

"She's taking drawing classes. She wants to be an ar-chitect. Maybe she'll make a lot of money."

"Architects don't make a lot of money," Hattie said. "And anyway, you shouldn't be worrying your head over money."

"She has a gift," Ms. Dell said. "All of you Torys have gifts. You with your writing, your mama with her draw-ings, and remember the things your daddy did with wood. Oh, that man was something else!"

"What's Li'l Jay's going to be?"

Ms. Dell stood up and pressed Li'l Jay's face to her cheek.

"Time's gonna tell us, Margaret. Now, come inside and do your homework while I fix you something to eat. No use sitting out in the cold."

Margaret rose and followed them inside.

"You hear anything from Maizon yet?" Hattie asked.

Margaret shook her head. If only Maizon were running up the block!

"I wrote her two letters and she hasn't written me one. Maybe she knows we're not really best friends anymore." Margaret sighed. She had been right in thinking she and Maizon were only old friends now, not the friends they used to be. "Still, I wish I knew how she was doing," she said, turning away so Hattie wouldn't see the tears in her eyes.

"We all do, honey," Hattie said, taking Margaret's hand. "We all do."

↘ CHAPTER 11 ↙

Two weeks later, Margaret sat at the kitchen table, scribbling furiously into her diary. When she looked up, the clock on the kitchen wall said ten thirty. She couldn't believe she had spent three hours writing. She flipped back to where she had begun and counted. Fifteen pages! Margaret heard her mother's key in the lock and quickly stuffed the diary back into her bookbag.

"Margaret," her mother said, coming into the kitchen, "what are you doing up? It's after ten o'clock."

"I wanted to stay up to tell you the news," Margaret said. Her mother sat across from her. "Ms. Peazle entered my poem in a contest! If I win, I get scholarship money and I get to read it in front of the mayor!"

Ms. Tory smiled and Margaret almost laughed with

pleasure at the pride in her mother's eyes. "That's wonderful, Margaret," she said, rising to give Margaret a hug.

Margaret shivered a little. They had never sat like this before, just the two of them in the soft quiet light of the kitchen. The feeling was new and strange. She felt closer to her mother all of a sudden. And the closeness felt grown-up and good.

"That would have made your daddy proud," her mother said softly.

Margaret swallowed. She hadn't thought about her father all day and now, looking away from the sadness in her mother's eyes, she saw her father clearly, smiling proudly down at her.

"He is proud, Mama," Margaret whispered. "From his place in heaven, he's real proud."

Her mother shook her head and dabbed at her eyes quickly, then rose. "Want to have some tea with me to celebrate?" she asked, going over to the stove. Not waiting for an answer, she put the teabags in cups and turned on the fire beneath the kettle. "You hear anything from Maizon?"

Margaret looked down at the table. The cloth blurred a little. Maizon had left a month ago. She shook her head.

Her mother turned back to the stove and poured the water into the cups. "I guess Blue Hill must be pretty hard. It's not like Maizon not to let anyone know how she's doing." She brought the cups over to the table. Margaret blew at the cloud of steam above her cup. "Have you spoken to her grandmother? Maybe she's heard something."

76

Margaret shook her head again. "I haven't been by there since Maizon left." All of a sudden she felt guilty. "It would just make me miss her more."

"She must be pretty lonely in that big house by herself," her mother said, reading her thoughts.

Margaret took a small sip of tea. It was minty and almost bitter. "I'll go see her after school tomorrow."

The kitchen fell silent. "You think Maizon forgot about Madison Street, Mama?"

Her mother laughed a little uncertainly. "It would take a lot to forget Madison Street."

"I was talking to some girls in school and they said they like me better since Maizon left. They said she was bossy and snotty."

Her mother looked up. "What did you say to them?"

Margaret picked nervously at the vinyl checkered tablecloth. The small hole wore away to a bigger one.

"Don't, Margaret," her mother said gently.

"I didn't say anything," she admitted.

"Don't let them say bad things about her when she's not here to defend herself. That's not what a real friend would do."

Margaret swallowed and took a quick sip of tea. The hot liquid washed the sadness back down for a moment.

"I wanted to tell them that Maizon's not like that, that they didn't know her like I did," she said quietly.

Her mother laid her hand on top of Margaret's. "Why didn't you? It's not like you not to."

Margaret shrugged. "The words got stuck. Those girls never paid any attention to me. I wanted them to keep liking me. I don't hardly have any friends in school." She looked up at her mother helplessly. "I felt real bad when I walked away, though."

Her mother shook her head. "It's hard to know what to do," she said, almost to herself. "I miss your father and I want to talk about him with a friend sometimes, but then I don't want anyone to remind me how empty I feel." She sniffed and gave Margaret a weak smile. "You better get to bed. School tomorrow."

"You okay, Mama?" She felt as though a strong wind had blown in between them, pulling them further and further apart. The closeness she had felt a moment ago was gone.

"It's going to take time, Margaret. Everything will fall into place. But it's going to take time."

Margaret hugged her. "We have a lot of time, Mama."

CHAPTER 12

"IT MUST be scary for Maizon up there," Grandma said. She sat in her armchair gazing out the window. In the October wind, yellow and gold leaves pressed themselves for quick moments to the window, then hurried off again.

"Guess it must seem to her like a long time ago she was smart," Ms. Dell said. She sat across from Grandma on the overstuffed couch. "Now she's just one of a lot of smart girls caught up there in that Connecticut school, inching along. Guess it's hard no longer being the smartest one . . ."

"She's still probably the smartest one," Margaret said.

Ms. Dell shook her head. "She'd have dropped us some kind of note if that was the case. Here it is already a month and some weeks gone by."

"Aren't you worried, Grandma? Maybe something happened."

Grandma continued to gaze out the window. When she finally spoke, her voice was soft. "When I took Maizon to Blue Hill, it seemed like what she wanted most was for me to leave so she could be on her own. So I left quickly. You know how Maizon is, Margaret. She's an individualist. I can't say she's a loner, because she needs people so much. And I know I spoil her. So I left and waited for her to call. I waited a week, then I called Blue Hill to see if there was anything wrong. They said everything was fine and Maizon was adjusting. I thought I should leave her to her adjusting and wait to hear from her. Sometimes I want to just go there and surprise her but I think that would be the wrong thing to do. I miss her so."

Margaret felt her chest press down and rise up in her throat. "How could she just forget about us? It's like she doesn't even remember me. I keep writing and writing . . ."

"It's hard up there, Margaret," Ms. Dell said reassuringly. "We thought Maizon forgot too."

Grandma nodded in agreement and Ms. Dell continued. "We thought what need does Maizon have with two old ladies—one who raised her, one who just raised eyes at her. But then after we talked some, thought about things a little, it made some sense to us. No, Margaret, she ain't the smartest girl no more. And you know Maizon. It's going to have to be a little snow on the ground in July before she let on that she ain't."

"She should just come home," Margaret said.

"Hattie found a job yesterday," Ms. Dell said quickly.

Margaret looked at her. Why was she changing the subject? "Say she gonna go back to school at night, get some degree or another."

"That would be nice," Grandma said. "Real nice." She turned to Margaret. "Maizon would think she failed all of us if she came home—"

"I wouldn't care," Margaret cut in. "If she hated that school and wanted to leave it, she should. . . ." Her voice trailed off.

"Maizon has to find her own way, Margaret," Grandma said.

"How are those new tenants?" Ms. Dell asked.

"Somebody else lives in this house now?" Margaret looked up. "Where? Who?"

"On the third floor," Grandma said. "I rented that apartment to a nice young man and his wife. You know Bettie. I made her wedding dress. No sense in staying in this big old house all alone."

"The money will be a help, I suppose."

Grandma waved her hand. "My husband provided for me. But those sounds, you know?"

Ms. Dell nodded. "Sounds of emptiness. Oh, do I know. Floors creaking and nobody walking on them. Windows falling shut after being open for days. Make you crazy!"

Margaret leaned back against the wall, surprised at how calm she felt. The house was the same house even if new people were living upstairs, she thought. She listened to them talk quietly about things that didn't matter much to her. But the sound of their conversation, soft and slow as a dance, blended in with the other neighborhood sounds. Someone was trying to get a car started. Next door, someone swept leaves out onto the curb. Margaret closed her eyes for a moment and the sounds faded. Behind her lids, Maizon was home and it was last summer again.

CHAPTER 13

"MARGARET! Hey, Margaret, wait up!"

Margaret spun around to see Bo Douglas racing toward her. Even though the temperature had dropped in the last few weeks, Bo still wore a T-shirt and carried his jacket. He leaped over a pile of leaves and grinned as he got closer.

"You walk pretty fast!" he said, catching his breath. "I've been trying to catch up with you for a block!" He had never been this close to her before and Margaret glanced nervously at his smooth brown skin and square jaw. He was at least a foot taller than her. "I heard your poem won a prize in the all-city poetry contest. Congratulations!"

"Th-Thanks," Margaret stuttered. "I knew Ms. Peazle

had entered it in the contest, but I didn't think it would win!"

Bo stuck out his hand and Margaret stared at it for a moment. Was she supposed to shake it? She shifted her books awkwardly and touched it with her own.

"Thank you," she said again.

"Well, we might as well walk to school together since we're both headed that way," Bo said shyly. He pulled the stark white T-shirt away from his neck as if it were uncomfortable, and brushed something invisible off the creased blue jeans he was wearing. They stopped short, above new-looking basketball sneakers.

"Are you coming to the assembly today?" Margaret asked.

"Can't you see I'm dressed up for it? This is as dressed up as the Bo gets," he laughed.

Margaret blushed.

"Aren't you nervous about reading your poem in front of all those people, Margaret?"

"No . . . not yet. I guess when I get onstage I will be, though. Anyway, this is just like a practice, sort of."

"When do you read it at city hall?"

"The day before Thanksgiving. My mother's taking the day off, and Ms. Dell and Hattie—they're my neighbors— are coming too."

Bo shook his head. "I doubt if I could ever do anything that good—that the mayor would want to see."

"I bet you could play basketball real well."

Bo stopped suddenly. "We might make it to the play-offs this season." He faked a dribble and took a shot into the air. Margaret wondered how he could move so much and still hold on to the three books he was carrying. "If we do, you want to come?"

"To watch you play?" She felt the heat rise in her face again. "Sure." She hoped Bo didn't want to shake on it. Her hands were drenched with sweat.

"Cool!"

They turned into the school yard.

"Hey, Margaret," Bo said, heading toward a group of basketball buddies, "I'll give you a wave when you go up onstage."

"Okay."

"See you later."

"Bye," Margaret said, staring at his back as he walked away. Wait until Maizon hears about this! She stopped to say hello to a group of girls in her class before rushing off to the auditorium.

Ms. Peazle had said it would be okay, this once, to meet the class in the auditorium. When the first-period bell rang, Margaret hid behind the curtain and watched as the students filed in.

"Just relax," Ms. Peazle whispered, coming up behind her. But looking out over the auditorium only made her tremble more. She hid until the principal introduced her.

Margaret couldn't remember ever being this nervous. Her heart raced between her mouth and stomach. Then faces began to come into focus and Margaret recognized friends from last year when she was in 5–2. None of them had made it to 6–1 with her. She put the poem on the podium and counted to ten as Ms. Dell had suggested.

Her breath slowed and when she opened her mouth, the words of the poem spilled out freely.

"My pen doesn't write anymore," she began. Her voice filled up every crevice in the auditorium and she liked the way it sounded.

When she finished, Margaret expected the same silence that had followed when she read in class. But the auditorium rumbled with applause. Some people were even standing. A few whistled. In the back, Bo's long brown hand waved back and forth.

"We should all be very proud of Margaret," Ms. Peazle said once the class had settled back in their room. "She has shown us the true meaning of being in 6–1. This is an honor given only to students who have shown that they are willing to work hard and do their best. I'd like to congratulate not only Margaret, but to congratulate all of you!"

The class cheered.

Margaret eased her plaque into her schoolbag. She didn't want the kids to think she was showing off or anything.

After school, Margaret walked home slowly. Clouds hung low in the sky and a cold wind blew down Madison Street. The brownstones looked gray and cold. Margaret stopped at the stoop and looked toward the compromise spot. Most of the leaves had fallen off the tree. She entered her building and tapped lightly on Ms. Dell's door. It was unlocked.

"Anyone comin' in must be a friend, 'cause we ain't

got anything here crooks would want or strangers would care to see," Ms. Dell always said.

"Margaret, it's sure good to see you," Ms. Dell said, coaching a spoonful of chopped green beans into Li'l Jay's mouth. He was in a bad mood and wouldn't eat. "This baby has been hollering all day. Maybe he'll hush now that you're here. I'm getting too old for this," she said tiredly.

"How did the reading go?" Hattie asked from the kitchen window as she dusted a framed picture of a younger Ms. Dell.

"Great! And guess what," Margaret said, watching Li'l Jay play with his beans.

"What?"

"People cheered. Everybody cheered!"

"Well, what did you expect them to do?" Ms. Dell asked, winking at Hattie.

The phone rang.

"Hello?" Hattie said. There was a long pause. "Yes, operator. I'll accept the charges." She handed the phone to Margaret.

"Who is it?" Margaret mouthed.

"It's for you."

"Hello?" Margaret said. There was a lot of static on the line and the voice sounded tiny and far away.

"Maizon?"

≼ CHAPTER 14 ≽

MARGARET hung up the phone and frowned. Ms. Dell took one look at her and sat down. They stared at each other silently.

"She's coming home, isn't she?"

Margaret nodded. She looked around the kitchen, wondering what she should do with her hands. Her conversation with Maizon ran crazily through her mind.

"Coming home!" Hattie said. "It's hasn't even been three months."

"She's coming home," she repeated, and began chewing on her cuticle.

"Sit down, Margaret," Ms. Dell said.

Margaret kneeled beside her and rested her chin on Ms. Dell's thighs. They were warm and soft beneath the corduroy skirt she wore.

"She said . . ." Margaret began, then frowned. The words had disappeared as quickly as they had come.

"Think about it a moment," Hattie said, taking a seat at the other end of the table.

Margaret felt her heart constrict into a small, painful lump. She took a breath and continued.

"I should be happy, right?" She looked up at Ms. Dell, biting her lip to keep from crying. "I should be happy she's coming home."

"You feel what you feel, Margaret."

"She said they hate her there."

"Who hates her?" Hattie said softly.

"She said the other girls. No one speaks to her."

"Now, Margaret," Hattie said calmly. "You know how Maizon can exaggerate some things sometimes . . ."

"No, Hattie," Margaret said quickly, "I heard it in her voice. I heard the way she was feeling." She looked at Ms. Dell for encouragement. Ms. Dell nodded. "She wasn't lying."

"I could feel it, Hattie." Margaret began to cry. "She wants me to tell her grandmother." She wiped her eyes with the back of her hand and looked up. "She thinks her grandmother doesn't want her back."

Ms. Dell sucked her teeth. "That's just foolishness."

Margaret sighed and stood up. Her stomach felt like it had a thousand tiny men marching in it. She thought about Maizon's voice. It had been soft and painful as a bruise.

"I gotta go talk to Grandma. Do you mind staying with Li'l Jay awhile longer?"

"Jay go!" Li'l Jay shouted, struggling to free himself from the highchair.

Hattie nodded.

Margaret pulled her coat on, then stood at the door for a moment. She turned back to Li'l Jay.

"I gotta go, Jay. She's my best friend. Best friends are best friends always," Margaret said, pulling the door closed behind her. "No matter what."

"Isn't it just like Maizon to make her do the dirty work?" she heard Hattie say.

⚰ CHAPTER 15 ⚰

GRANDMA brought two cups of tea into the living room and handed one to Margaret. It smelled of cinnamon and oranges. Margaret blew on it and continued to stare out the window. A streetlamp flickered on, lighting up the small evergreen Grandma had set out.

"I've been thinking about you, Margaret."

Margaret turned to her. "I've been thinking about you too. I'm sorry I haven't come by since the last time, when Ms. Dell was here."

Grandma waved her hand. "Oh, I know how school is these days. Keeps you so busy, I'm surprised I'm getting to see you again before June." She took a sip and looked past Margaret out the window. "I suppose Maizon is pretty busy too. I haven't heard much from her at all."

Margaret swallowed and Grandma continued.

"Just little notes here and there." She lifted her shoulders. "But how can I fault her? Blue Hill is challenging, I suppose."

"Maybe it's too challenging, Grandma."

Grandma smiled. She looked faraway. "Not for my Maizon," she said proudly. "She's a survivor if I ever saw one."

Margaret nodded.

"She still believes her daddy's going to come back someday. And who knows, maybe he will. But I stopped believing in him the day he left my daughter to die."

"How did she die, Grandma?" Margaret asked, hoping to avoid the subject of Blue Hill for as long as she could.

"Giving birth to Maizon," Grandma said, a little surprised. "Maizon never told you that?"

Margaret shook her head. The men were back in her stomach again.

"No, no. Of course she wouldn't. I think Maizon blames herself. She blames herself for everything, it seems. She covers it up, though. She tries to be brave and— What's the word you kids use these days?" She frowned for a moment, then looked at Margaret again. "Cool. Every time I turn around, she's telling me about the latest something."

"I used to think Maizon knew everything, Grandma," Margaret said. "Now I know she doesn't."

"Nobody does, Margaret."

"I know. . . . Now I know."

They looked at each other for a moment. Grandma smiled.

"What is it, Margaret?" she asked.

Margaret felt the tears well up in her throat again. She looked down at her tea. A small dark mass had collected at the bottom of her cup. She swished it around absently, thinking about her conversation with Maizon.

"Maizon's coming home," she said finally, looking up at Grandma. "She called me at Ms. Dell's just now."

"She wants to leave the school?"

Margaret nodded and wrapped her hands around the cup. The tea was growing cold. "She says they don't treat her like a human there. She says she's not happy."

"But why didn't she call me, Margaret? Doesn't she know she can talk to her grandmother?"

Margaret didn't know how to answer. For a second, she hated Maizon for making her do this.

"She was scared, Grandma."

"Scared?"

"That you would think she's a failure or something."

Grandma gazed out at her evergreen. "She can never fail me, Margaret."

Margaret wanted to tell Grandma how important it was to Maizon to come home now, how she needed Madison Street and her and Ms. Dell and especially Grandma to understand. But when she looked up, Grandma was smiling slowly, like she knew already and it was all right.

"How come Maizon can still surprise me?" She raised a hand, palm flat out toward the ceiling, and sighed.

Margaret laughed a little. It seemed like the first time she'd laughed in a long time and the sound felt good against the quiet.

"Margaret . . ."

Margaret looked up. Thick tears spilled from the corners of Grandma's eyes. Margaret darted to the couch and reached for her hand. The skin was dry and warm.

"I missed her, Margaret. I'm glad she'll be coming home."

"Me too, Grandma."

❧ CHAPTER 16 ❧

Margaret pulled a chair to the window and looked out toward the bridge. It was too warm for November. Indian summer is what Ms. Dell had called it. Maizon would be sitting by the train window now, watching the white Connecticut snow turn gray, then yellow, as the train neared the city. New York would seem dirty and overcast.

"Connecticut smells like grass and rain even after the last grass has died," Margaret wrote in the legal pad she used as a diary now that her old one was full. "New York air is gray and still."

Jay crept up beside her.

"Pow!" he said, pointing a finger at her head.

Margaret ignored him and kept writing. "The buildings

rush by in blurs of gray and red brick. Below, hundreds of cars move slowly."

"Word," Jay said, pointing to the pad.

"Writer," Margaret said, pointing to herself. She turned to a clean page and continued. "Just like Ms. Peazle said I should be. She says I have a gift, Jay."

Li'l Jay giggled and ran to the window.

"You can laugh if you want to. But just wait," Margaret said, bending back down over her diary and continuing to write. "Yesterday, Mama came into the living room and hugged me for no reason at all. She said it was the first day since Daddy died that she hadn't cried. I hugged her back hard. I feel Daddy's spirit in this house. Every time the wind blows the curtains against the walls, every time I hear Li'l Jay laugh in his sleep or Mama singing, I know Daddy is here."

"May-za," Li'l Jay said.

Margaret didn't look up. "She's coming home today. Her grandmother went to get her. You have to be patient," she said. The butterflies in her stomach had turned to bats and time had stopped moving four hours ago. It seemed like nearly three years, not three months since she had last seen Maizon. "Bo is even going to drop by tomorrow to say 'hi'! Imagine! Bo Douglas in my house!"

"May-za!" Li'l Jay said again, running over to Margaret. He patted her on the arm and pointed to the window.

"May-za!"

Margaret looked toward the window.

"You want to see out?"

Li'l Jay nodded and ran back over to the window. Margaret sighed and laid the pad and pencil on the chair, then lifted Li'l Jay up.

"May-za!" Li'l Jay said, pointing down the street.

Margaret put Li'l Jay down and raised the window. Maizon was pulling her gate closed and heading up the block.

"Maizon!" She yelled. Maizon waved and ran the rest of the way. Margaret rushed into her coat and slammed out the door. When she got to the top of the last flight, she stopped. Li'l Jay had known before he saw her!

"Mama, Maizon's back!" she called over her shoulder, rushing out of the building.

Margaret ran down the street and met her halfway. "Maizon! Li'l Jay is like Ms. Dell! He got her gift!"

THE MOMENT they sat down under their tree, Margaret knew there was something different about Maizon. It was more than the fact that Maizon had grown even taller or that she had let her Afro get too long. Margaret stared at her. When Maizon looked up, Margaret saw the pain in her eyes. There was something about the look that was familiar but she couldn't remember where she had seen it before.

"I hated it there, Margaret," Maizon said softly.

Before she could finish, Margaret recognized the look. It was the same one Hattie had—sad and faraway even when she laughed. It was a look that said something had been broken, something that could never be fixed.

"What did they do to you?" Margaret asked, leaning

against Maizon's shoulder. It felt as warm and bony as it always had.

"They hated me because I'm black and smart."

"They said that to you?!" Margaret raised her head and looked at Maizon. "That's the meanest . . ."

"They didn't exactly say it, Margaret. They didn't have to. Everything they did showed it. For three months I ate alone, slept in a room by myself, worked by myself, and everything."

"They were all like that?"

"No." Maizon looked at her palms. She made a fist and looked up at the sprinkling of leaves left on the tree. "Some of them tried to be nice. There were a couple of other black girls there too. Sometimes they talked to me but not much. I don't know why. I guess because I didn't try to talk to them either. I think they thought I was stuck-up. But I wanted to find a friend like you, Margaret, someone I could tell everything to."

"Why didn't you write me then, Maizon? I was still here in Brooklyn all the time." Margaret smiled a little, trying to hide the hurt in her voice. The smile stopped before it reached her eyes.

"I'm sorry," Maizon said, sounding afraid. "I didn't want you to know how hard it was. I wanted you to think everything was okay."

"You still should have written."

Maizon sniffed and looked out over the block. "I missed you so much, Margaret. And I missed Ms. Dell and Li'l Jay, even Hattie."

"Let's walk over to Palmetto Street," Margaret said,

rising and taking Maizon's hand. "The leaves falling off this tree are starting to get to me."

"Me too."

They walked in silence.

"I guess I didn't write because I didn't want you to think there was stuff I couldn't do," Maizon said, sitting on the curb across from the new apartment building. Margaret sat beside her. "When I read your poem I was so happy and so jealous at the same time. I felt like you had everything, Margaret."

"Everything?"

"You had Madison Street and Ms. Dell and your mother, even my grandmother. All I had was Connecticut and a bunch of strangers."

"I missed you, Maizon! I didn't have a best friend anymore! I didn't have anyone to tell how much I missed Daddy or to walk home with from school. Li'l Jay can barely make sentences and Ms. Dell, well, she knows stuff, so I can't really tell her anything new."

Maizon smiled and nodded. "I'm glad I came home, Margaret."

"Me too. Anyway, Ms. Peazle isn't so bad."

"I can't go back to 102," Maizon said. "Not now. Not after Blue Hill and everything."

"So what are you going to do?" Margaret asked. When Maizon didn't respond, she followed her gaze. Three stories above, in the new apartment building, a blond girl pressed her face against the window, staring down at them.

"Who's she?" Maizon asked.

"I don't know. She just moved in. I can see her staring all the time from my window."

"Does she go to 102?"

"No," Margaret said. "A bus picks her up. It says Pace Academy on the side."

"Probably just like Blue Hill!" Maizon said, frowning at the girl.

"I don't think it is, Maizon. Ms. Dell talked to her mother at the store. The school's for gifted children in New York. It's free for everyone, not just people on scholarship or whatever. Ms. Dell said Mama should sign me up."

"For real, Margaret?"

Margaret nodded. "It's a new school. Sort of like an experiment or something, to see how kids from different areas act around each other."

"Maybe I could go there, Margaret."

"Me too!"

Maizon jumped up. "Maybe it could be just like it was before I went away"—she hesitated—"almost."

Margaret read her thoughts. "Ms. Dell says people change. Maybe it can't be exactly like it was."

"I know I changed, Margaret. I changed because Blue Hill was so hard."

"But, Maizon, you're the smartest girl in Brooklyn. . . ."

"Not book hard," Maizon cut in. "Those classes were a breeze. Just the people . . ." Her voice trailed off and she looked up toward the window again.

"Not everyone is like that, Maizon."

"I know," Maizon said. "A couple of teachers at Blue Hill were nice to me. And the lady who worked in the cafeteria almost cried when I told her I was leaving. Some of the girls looked sad when they saw me packing."

The blond girl waved and smiled.

Margaret waved back. "She's probably lonely like you were."

"Yeah," Maizon said. She took one last look, then turned away.

"Maybe someday we can invite her over and show her the bridge, Maizon."

Maizon nodded.

They walked slowly down Palmetto Street. A cold wind blew in between them and lifted Maizon's hair. They giggled and chased the brown and gold leaves scattering themselves along the block.

"If you find a gold one with a little yellow in it," Maizon yelled from across the street, "it means we'll be friends forever!"

"I'm going to find a million gold ones!" Margaret yelled back. She watched Maizon's Afro dance in the wind. In the fading afternoon sun, she danced and said, "A million, trillion, zillion gold ones!"

About the Author

JACQUELINE WOODSON grew up in Brooklyn, where *Last Summer with Maizon,* her first novel, is set. She says: "Ms. Dell and Hattie and Maizon and Margaret are all people I would like to have known in my childhood. I think I want to know what happened to Maizon at Blue Hill. And where did Ms. Dell and her magic come from? For me, *Last Summer with Maizon* is only the beginning of all this.

"I want to keep on writing for children of color. And when they're finished reading what I have written, I want Maizon and Margaret and everyone on Madison Street to visit readers again."

Jacqueline Woodson is a drama therapist who works in a New York City residence for runaway and homeless children between the ages of ten and seventeen.